In An Oubliette

Jean Andrews

Published 2005 by arima publishing

www.arimapublishing.com

ISBN 1-84549-066-5

© Jean Andrews 2005

All rights reserved

This book is copyright. Subject to statutory exception and to provisions of relevant collective licensing agreements, no part of this publication may be reproduced, stored in a retrieval system, or transmitted in any form or by any means, without the prior written permission of the author.

Printed and bound in the United Kingdom

Typeset in Verdana 12/16

This book is sold subject to the conditions that it shall not, by way of trade or otherwise, be lent, re-sold, hired out, or otherwise circulated without the publisher's prior consent in any form of binding or cover other than that which it is published and without a similar condition including this condition being imposed on the subsequent purchaser.

arima publishing
ASK House, Northgate Avenue
Bury St Edmunds, Suffolk IP32 6BB
t: (+44) 01284 700321

www.arimapublishing.com

My thanks, profound and longstanding, to Máire Holmes, Feargal Murray and Elizabeth Taylor.

A Note

Leandra's first line came to me out of nowhere in August of nineteen eighty nine and pursued me until I wrote it down.

This was before the fall of the Berlin Wall, the release of Nelson Mandela, the internecine conflict in the former Yugoslavia, the genocide in Rwanda, the rise of transnational terrorism, global warming, mobile phones and the internet age.

I'm sorry to say it has taken me all those years to figure out what might have happened to her, and even then I'm not entirely sure.

In any case, her story belongs to that time of my own innocence and the world as it was then, in that Summer of nineteen eighty nine.

1

Leandra

I came back,
only when I was ready to leave again,
to the town of my latest, my most profound defeat.

It was an austere town, proud and medieval,
set atop a steep and windblown hill.

Cathedral and castle glowered there,
out across the centuries,
out into the Northern Chill.

2

St Ethelreda's Cathedral, Copplestone Keep

The cathedral squints across sullen seas,
the castle sits
on the northerly breeze.
I lived and worked in an edifice
squeezed in
between both of these.

A house that once was an apothecary's.
In a time of Enlightenment,
and gravitation towards secular ways.

I should have known that there would also be,
in this scheme of things,
a meeting of waters, an end of the days.

3

John Fairbright, apothecary

In Queen Anne's time, I had a sliver of a building
    inserted
in the crack between Copplestone Keep, ten ninety-
    six,
squat and square-jawed as any Norman crusader,
and the prissy, blackened mass
which was now St Ethelreda's Cathedral,
named for a Saxon virgin, martyr and saint,
cheek-by-jowl, a long time since,
with a second, outland invader.

I was determined to bring about the new:
science, order and method,
empirical observation;
the conclusion that all that Man could know
and depend upon
was Man.

In view of which,
in cloth-bound ledgers, to the last half crown,
the toll of our Enlightenment
would continue to be handed down.

4

Miss Corinna Fairbright

I held on, dear, into my eighties.
Then I let the place to a dealer in antiquities,
withdrew to what is now called
"sheltered" accommodation,
as if its purpose were not yet
thoroughly understood.

Fairbright's the Chemists?
Why, that was over by the fifties,
I had no liking for study,
nor for marriage to one who had,
so, I played to my strengths
and sold toys instead.

But, I kept the custom of the ledgers:
all those children whose Christmas
was better than their parents could make it.

In the end, however, it took every penny I had.

Now one rent pays for another.
This antique in exchange, you see,
for those others.

5

Leandra

One day,
it had been, up to then,
quite an ordinary day,
in the last grey Summer
of the Cold War,
the plaster still intact
on the Berlin Wall,
when a caller I had never seen before
brought me some miniature soldiers
his wife's brother had bequeathed.

He knew nothing about them
wondered if he sold them
would it be - he mumbled -
too vulgar an act
in his hour of grief.

They were pristine miniatures from the Napoleonic
 Wars,
and all accounted for
in their original tin boxes,
Brittain pieces all.

It was perfectly normal,
I assured him,
and he could leave them with me.

6

Alkaios, seller

I am over sixty now,
but time does not remove the scars.

The years I was a lunatic, I cannot count.

I only know I came to sentience the day
I saved the life of a Tommy in a mangled truck.

It was hurled by a landmine down a ravine.

Of the seven casualties within her,
he was the only one with any passing luck.

7

Leandra

I am not a fanciful woman.
Indeed, I have been all my life
a creature of calm and Austen-like persuasion.

Those soldiers were merely tin toys,
after all,
and not in any way to be blamed
for the madness that appeared
to overtake me.

There had to be a sensible,
rational explanation.

8

Alkaios

I learned his language, helped him communicate in
 mine,
and followed when he left, to his far country.

There, I wed his wayward sister
when she needed a husband
and respite
from misadventures with Yankee GIs.

I needed shelter,
and she was, in those first months,
solicitous, sometimes even kind.

But she lost the child,
and from then on ceased to care.

Her forays resumed
and ranged both far and wide:
men, women,
for her there was no such thing
as a gender divide.

Yet, what business was it of mine?

I had given her respectability,
she claimed little else from me besides.

So, all the while, I made what I could
of the remaining fragments of my life.

9

Anthony, rescued Tommy.

In nineteen forty seven,
the toy soldiers
were all that was left
of what I had held
most unutterably dear.

At what I knew would have been her behest,
I kept them near,
and then got on, like everyone else,
with the formalities of life
in the wake of her death,
and so many other deaths,
and my own return
from what has been known,
Heaven help us,
since time immemorial,
as the theatre of war.

Enid

We might have married
if it weren't for that Godforsaken car.
Who dies in a prosaic, civilian accident
in the midst of world-engulfing war?

I secreted the toy soldiers,
once my late husband's, in unsuspecting Anthony's
        care:
Napoleonic guards and lancers,
cuirassiers, hussars.
All spotless from the furnace,
shabraques and scimitars,
with gold-and-lace fieldmarshals
conducting re-enactments
of the squalour
and the spectacle
of the theatre of war.

11

Arnold Blackstaffe, Mayor

I am the last Blackstaffe that I know of
living in these parts.

I have no children and no kindred near.

Even so, I am in my fifties now
and have neither fallen
to accident nor tubercular infection.

Among the men of my family,
I count myself extraordinary.

My wife will survive me, no doubt,
she is considerably younger,
and women do live a deal longer.

The war will inevitably come,
in spite of appeasement.
The idolatry of demagogues
to which our age appears
peculiarly susceptible,
will have it so.
In reaction against which,
in this age of waiting uncertainty,
I have honoured my grandfather's wish,
and left his tin soldiers embargoed:
Napoleonically, alone.

My wife,

when the time comes,
I am certain of it,
will be less willingly forsworn.

12

Rory Fergusson, Laird.

They wouldn't leave me be. Hah!
Wasn't it enough to lose my son?
So I packed them off
to dotty, dear old Jamie Blackstaffe.

God knows what he made of them.
He was much more worried about that blasted
Priest in the Hole.

13

James Blackstaffe, recusant.

The curse on Black Lewis was enough for me.
They say the evil prosper,
it's those who come after them who have to pay.
His loyal, Royalist brother Morris killed by a plough
just six months after that unforgiving priest
        expired,
while he went onto marry thrice,
father three times that and many more
on the other side of the blanket,
and die snoring beyond fourscore
in his ill-gotten bed,
a Catholic once again,
just to hedge his bets.

And every last one of us since then
slain before our time
by some misgotten malady,
all except me,
and Rory Fergusson has to send
those accursed tin soldiers
the ruination of his peace and his grieving
since his son's death at Mafeking,
his time spent rehearsing the tactics over and over
        again
until the man went nearly out of his head.

I haven't unloosed them,
nor shall I,
they remain in their boxes,

forever sealed.
I have enough to contend with,
in the curse of Father Shields.

14

Father Shields, Jesuit.

I never thought I'd die
unhouseled, unanneled
in a smoky oubliette,
in the dark
with a sputtering candle
long extinguished
while a young man
with no harm in him
at that point, it is true,
followed the rising sap
and plucked another flower
from the serpent's tree.

Nor did I think,
until my last breath,
that I would have
the rancour in me
to curse him
and all his progeny
to Kingdom Come.

I pray for it now, of course,
in disappointment at myself
and remorse.

15

Leandra

I was only the conduit for a
commercial transaction,
strictly speaking,
after all.

And I did not ask them to appear to me.
Certainly not.
And I ought to have remained to them
as invisible as I was,
to almost all my clientele.

I should never have become
part of their rules of engagement.

But still they came,
with their innocuous, yet well-meaning,
platitudinous advice.
Set fair even so
on the ruination,
of one amid many others,
of my insignificant life.

I told them.
War is not for me to do.

I leave that,
to the officer class and their minions,
all those millions
since consciousness began.

16

Enid

I lifted the lid, of course I did.

Who would believe it?

To be addressed, though a woman, as an equal by Fieldmarshal Kutuzov and Napoleon!

Who would miss such an opportunity?

17

Murat, sometime king of Naples

I was a peacock and a popinjay
and, by God, was I made for disport and display!

18

Leandra

Oh God, even when I confine them to the cellar
they come upon me, in the night,
at the foot of my bed,
with their pride
and their sense of things mislaid.

For this and much else
I am not, have never been,
made.

19

Murat

Oh, and by the way...
in case you believe those false reports.

In the fifteenth century women routinely went to
war
and served as loaders for the tiny artillery used in
sieges.

In our time, they served respectably as
vivandières,
less so as voyeurs, camp followers, and whores.

There were times when the Grande Armée
had almost as many civilians as fighting men, in
tow.
Tedious, tiresome but nonetheless distracting.

Don't let any woman tell you she has no concept of
war.
She and her sisters know everything there is to
know,
that and probably far, far more.

20

Rory Fergusson

They did, the bastards, they spoke to me.
Why couldn't it have been Nelson or Wellington
or, God bless his weak-kneed, inbred socks and
 sporran,
the King Over the Water himself?

What did I want with Bagration or Murat or, for that
 matter, Ney,
one I could respect at least,
or Poniatowski whose predicament, of all,
I could condole with?

21

Kutuzov

In what, I'm fully aware,
has become my legendarily lumbering way,
I will nonetheless take this opportunity to say
that patience and time are still
the solutions to everything,
hard though they may be to tolerate,
let alone acquire.

When I waited for the Emperor Napoleon to reach
    Moscow
I was an old man.
In the eyes of many, already as good as dead,
useless and out to grass.
But, with the eye,
my eye, not taken by an Ishmaili bullet,
I knew the Winter would be no different in eighteen
    twelve,
and it wasn't.
Many say it was considerably worse.

When it was all over
ordinary men took charge of matters not beyond
    their measure.
This too was right.
I withdrew to the life I had lived before.
My kind are only welcome
in time of war.

22

Napoleon

That battle of Borodino
which men hailed as a triumph of mine at the time
was, in reality, my swansong,
had I but known it.

I should have taken those damned Bagration
    flèches with ease,
I would have only a year or so before,
they say I dawdled and identify the first strains of
    lethargy,
of fallibility, my lack of a young man's confident
    stride.
Maybe so.
But those were not the fires then banking down
    within me,
it was that each attempt at control, at rendering
    sanity
met with constant, unremitting war,
and each battle begat another and each border
    crossed and conquered
shat another set of complications on my head.
What could I do but seek to end this madness
by overcoming all
and still, no matter what,
the system would not come to rest,
to equilibrium.
So, I tired, the pendulum
before the hands of the clock.
When it was over,

In An Oubliette

they should have shot me.
The warcrime was to let me live.

23

Ney

I did not think to see a land more riven with
    inequality
than mine own before the Revolution.
Lands under occupation one makes allowances for,
and the soldier in an invading army has a rather
    skewed view
I will admit. And yet.
Here I stand in scavenged motley,
between the Dnieper and the Don,
the *Grande Armée* all gone for manure, save a few.
Crops trampled, earth scorched, livestock
    slaughtered before us
on our victorious march to Moscow,
no clothes on our backs, no food in our guts,
no powder in our packs, noses, ears, digits frozen,
    rotted off,
and the putrid, perished remains of all matter
    animal and vegetable,
for greeting on our retreat
all this made more exquisite, as torturers say,
by shot, sabres, scimitars, garottings from behind.
    And yet.
Why was this land of tsars and boyars,
as bad as the worst of our *ancien régime*,
so worth defending?
I am shamed by this.

24

Poniatowski

Why did I do it?
The glory of entering Moscow a conqueror,
however short the reign and distasteful the rabble,
but the ill-educated, ill-bred cyclops of this so-
 called *Grande Armée*
knew only how to fight as if the next mouthful still
 depended on battle
when they should have sued for terms,
given Alexander a chastening and pulled back,
to die contentedly in their beds.
Ignorance has no measure of plenty,
I lost, we all lost, everything as a result.

Jean Andrews

25

Bagration

It was no way to die.
For a series of ephemera,
it took me seventeen days,
of agony.

Nor for *Joseph Antonievich,*
Prince Poniatowski, drowned
a year after my death
crossing the Dnieper.

We were neither of us Russians,
only *Mikhail Ilarionovich,*
Kutuzov to the world at large,
understood the true nature of it.

The rest, House of Bagration,
House of Poniatowski,
House of What You Like
on either side of a cosmetic divide,
doing what the older generation expects,
laying down our lives, losing our limbs
for some wholly untenable notion
of familial pride.

Though I lived into my forties,
a good age for the time and my occupation,
and Poniatowski was over fifty when he died,
I cannot see there was anything now
that much worth fighting for.

26

Kutuzov

We do what we must,
the rest is chance.
Explanation is the luxury
of those who survive,
though I understand
in your time,
it has come to be seen
as more of a cross to bear
than anything else.
I am with Tolstoy on this,
there is nothing we can do.
Only our best.

27

Diarmid Fergusson, soldier

In my day, it was what most promising young men
 did, those due to
inherit an estate in the fullness of time.
If one were lucky, one died years later, of gout and
 apoplexy, maybe,
but securely in ones bed.
If not, a solitary marble plaque, neo-classical in
 style, perhaps,
adorned the village church, complete with
 regimental flag.

I died of fever at Mafeking. Not of the exigencies of
 war. Matters rarely
given prominence in newspaper reports.
Had I lived, I might well have done some good in a
 serious way, even as
now I essay a sober propriety in my speech.
I was a thoughtless twenty-three when I
 succumbed, however, with no
idea of why a war had to be fought in the veldt.

And my father who sent me, with nothing but the
 most correct of
intentions, to follow in the ancient trodden path,
would, in other circumstances, in our ancestral
 circumstances, more
easily have supported the rival Boer,
in memory of and homage to Culloden and
 Bannockburn and many
other clashes more.

28

Leandra

If only I knew
how to get them back in their boxes.

I can't imagine that selling them will help.

They're no longer confined
and seem to be making a quagmire
of what's left
of what was,
once upon a time,
my crisp and businesslike mind.

29

Frederick Turnbull, buyer

Rory Fergusson was one of my maternal great-grandfathers.
I hadn't expected my antecedents to be of special importance,
that had been, after all, my wife's particular forte.

And who was I to compete with a Trevignac-Bonaparte?

30

Estella, historian

My family name was de Trevignac-Bonaparte.
I was descended from Napoleon's brother Jérôme,
His first wife was an American called Elizabeth
    Patterson.
They met and married in Baltimore.
Their grandson, Charles Joseph,
was US Secretary of the Navy
and Attorney General in the first decade
of the twentieth century.

History attracted me,
I don't know if it was because of the genes.
I went back to the warrior-monks,
who were supposedly celibate, impoverished
and obedient to the clarion call of the Church
    Militant
here on Earth.
I found
that they were greatly misconstrued.
Their everyday lives were harsh,
earnest and rough-hewn.

Those who weave Templar conspiracies
like UFOs to populate the skies
have no sense of the human business
these knights were about.
Many spoke to me
in testimony
and I, of course,

with my ancestor's visionary blood,
(a legacy come to rest
in more ways than one,
since a blood-borne illness,
in the end, carried me off),
believed them,
then used forensics for the eyes of the world.

Chief of these was Mordecai of Valence,
who will tell his own tale.

31

Mordecai, monk

I am Mordecai,
a Christian convert allowed to keep his Jewish
    name
in recompense for all that his family had suffered
in three pogroms:
Valence, then Paris, then York.

In Copplestone,
that square and squat fortress on a hill,
they took me in and the canons next door,
in the citadel of the Saxon martyr and virgin
    Ethelreda,
convinced me I had been spared three times
even as the cock crowed three times
for the weeping Saint Peter, no rock then,
to be about the business of God.

They left me my name and my history
as Simon Peter had been left his
and I became Mordecai of the Cross.
Later, I joined the Templars
in hope of seeing the Holy Land,
though I never got beyond Cyprus and died
years after, a victim of fortune,
pierced by a crossbow bolt
with and like Coeur de Lion
at the miserable rampart of Chalus,
fallen in the end to unholy war.

Jean Andrews

I left no mark on the world,
nor no child either,
I kept my vow
and could not show, in any case,
my circumcised prick
to any woman who might, afterwards,
seek to betray me.
But I spoke to Estella at Chalus
and she made my contribution to history,
I, it was, who gave her the last details
of Richard's final hours
and she gave it to all of you
for what is called posterity.

32

Alkaios

I leave nothing to the future,
not in my own, nor in my parents' name.

When I came back that day, I saw our vineyard
had been destroyed beyond reclaim,
burned, then smothered in quicklime.

They called themselves storm-troopers, from
          Bulgaria,
under orders to crush partisan support.
For what? In the fastness of Macedonia,
what difference could any of our actions make?

33

Leandra

So I sold them,
I didn't dare explain.
The buyer went off to Sydney,
with the figurines,
and they remained,
in this torture chamber,
with me.

You would think the letters
I found with them
might have been a greater curse:
intimation of such starstruck lives,
but they were not.
I just passed them back to that gentle old man,
with the sum the soldiers had earned.

And withdrew into my scarless torment,
ashamed of my impotence
in the face of his.

34

Alkaios

My brother-in-law was unlucky, yes,
and his sister, my wife, a minx, yes,
but these were small matters
in the sum total of things.

I was a boy full of sap and dreams,
out in the mountains, scouring for eagles' nests,
snakes and lizards or wildcats and bears,
which ended the day I came home
and found my parents charred,
and swinging from the eaves.

The Iron Guard.

My parents had been hiding soldiers,
in the barrels, among the lees,
a courage I knew nothing about,
until the neighbours told me, God knows how long
            after,
when I returned to my life and my senses,
and could pay heed,
though the Guard had done away with any
            possibility
of my ever sowing
any of my own seed.

Jean Andrews

35

Anthony

I would have married her at the end of the war.
While I doubted my own survival
I never contemplated any danger to hers.
My letters were returned to me sometime after her
    death.

Why did we keep it a secret?
In spite of the sexual laxity induced by the war,
class was still a major obstacle.
We came from the very opposite ends
of the social spectrum,
she was a well-to-do widow
and I a warehouseman ten years her junior.
I was her student at an evening class.

Afterwards, I gave people to understand
I had been fortunate to have been remembered
in Mrs Blackstaffe's will.

Diarmid Fergusson was in the Queen's Own
    Highlanders,
the traditional regiment of his family since
    Culloden.
His father started a collection of Brittain miniatures
the year Diarmid received his commission, eighteen
    ninety three,
taking a passionate interest in the Napoleonic
    Wars,
and siding, as far as possible, with the French.

Like many Highland families,
he was outwardly loyal to the Hanoverians
and their progeny,
but held true in memory
to the Stuart dream and the king-in-exile
over the water.

His son died on the day of the relief of Mafeking,
the seventeenth of May nineteen hundred.
From that day he believed the soldiers haunted him,
going over the Boer and British strategies
again and again, driving him to distraction.
So he sent them off to James Blackstaffe
who kept his old friend's bequest unopened
as Rory had dispatched it.
His son did the same and his grandson, Arnold,
after him.

But she was curious.
Not being a Blackstaffe by blood,
there was no Jesuit's curse.
So, when she needed an accomplice
it was me.
One day, we set them out:
artillery, cavalry, infantry,
field commanders and staff officers,
and finally, the generals,
and it became rapidly clear
that they were from the eighteen twelve campaign,
down to the hardiest Don Cossack,
and the most woebegone Portuguese mercenary.

When they were all in place she said,
"Well, what was there to be afraid of?
They're handsome, that's all."

Then, she swore she heard a voice:
No, my dear.
We will be from now on
a factor in your life,
until you die.
This will be a dilemma for you.

I neither saw nor heard them,
nor ever did,
but I believed her.

At one time, I wondered if they had distracted her
and been the cause of her accident,
but I put that long since from my mind,
for the sake of sanity.
She had the car only because of the hotel,
but maintenance was not a priority, she said.

Until the brakes failed,
and she was dead.

36

Leandra

I have had too much,
the soldiers are finally gone,
and I suffer now
from those awful gargoyles,
those leaning towers.
Squeezing the breath out of me
and my slender house.

I have no option,
I must leave.
They surely cannot cross the ocean
in my wake
and shatter the glasshouse of my sleep.

Jean Andrews

37

Copplestone and St Ethelreda's

We squeezed more than the breath out of her,
we crushed that suppository of a house.
It took us years.

We hadn't expected the generals,
we would have managed without them, it is true,
but they helped.

A two-pronged attack, the classic pincer
            manoeuvre:
we destroy her dwelling
while they invade her mind.

The old lady was dead,
fire took hold,
and the city council decreed
that the monstrous edifice
would not be rebuilt,
we were to be as we once were
free as the rushing breeze that coursed between us
on its way to the Northern seas.

38

Leandra

So I leave now
the town of my latest,
my most profound defeat.

I will never return.
This steep place,
with its tight cobbles and closed mind,
the arrow-slits squinting over the greyish sea
and the slate spire leering from on high,
a home no more to innocence,
this town is lost to me.

What evidence there ever was
that I was here
has now been obliterated
by fire and water,
and there remain only
gargoyles and crenellations,
the cutting winds and the driving rain.

I will stay no longer.
My house is gone,
there is no footprint of mine
any more.

And, like the swallow in winter,
I will fly south again,
and west,
towards the Sun,

towards the desert land
of nascent memory.

39

Frederick.

I am the man at the end of the line,
constrained by grief and the vortex of time.

I purchased the soldiers and paid a fair price,
expecting so little of the rest of my life.
Then sudden, headlong, giddy surprise:
I noticed the dealer.

Tearful, bedraggled, a Columbine,
I lured her to Sydney,
and made her my wife.

Cathedral and Castle

Most of you who stand there now
and pass judgement on us,
or, on your own terms,
offer an opinion,
with your modern consideration
for the comfort of the other,
you cannot have the remotest glimmer
of what we have seen and done.

We have witnessed every nation come and go:
the Normans and the Saxons, Picts,
displaced Celts and Norse,
they did their building
then buried their bones.
many of them,
in our inner and outer walls.
This is the way with every foundation.

We had technocrats,
from the dawn of our time,
purveyors of the filofax,
and believers,
with each new generation,
that humanity had finally found its way.
The Templars, the Roundheads,
that Godforsaken rationalist healer,
all came, and went.
But we are still the same.
And we are still here.

In An Oubliette

A squat-headed keep,
hewn of cathedral stone,
flesh from the same spindly bone,
as the Spartan, heavenward needle;
tower and spire,
eternally rising,
at one in the place
of the Everlasting Deep.

All else, you see, is dissipation.

www.ingramcontent.com/pod-product-compliance
Lightning Source LLC
Chambersburg PA
CBHW051718040426
42446CB00008B/940